Read & Re

FOR KS2

The Lion, the Witch and the Wardrobe

SECTION 2

Guided reading

SECTION 3

Shared reading

Plot, character and setting

Talk about it

Get writing

Assessment

Author: Celia Warren

Development Editor: Rachel Mackinnon

Editor: Sarah Sodhi

Assistant Editor: Louise Titley

Series Designer: Anna Oliwa

Designer: Liz Gilbert

Illustrations: Pauline Baynes

Designed using Adobe InDesign

Published by Scholastic Ltd,
Book End, Range Road, Witney,
Oxfordshire OX29 0YD
www.scholastic.co.uk

Printed by Bell & Bain

5 6 7 8 9 3 4 5 6 7 8

British Library Cataloguing-in-Publication Data
A catalogue record for this book is available from the British Library.
ISBN 978-1407-11400-2

Acknowledgements

The publishers gratefully acknowledge permission to reproduce the following copyright material: **The C. S. Lewis Company Ltd** for the use of text extracts and illustrations from *The Lion, the Witch and the Wardrobe* by C. S. Lewis text © 1950, C.S. Lewis Pte Ltd, illustrations by Pauline Baynes © 1950, C.S. Lewis Pte Ltd (2005, HarperCollins). Every effort has been made to trace copyright holders for the works reproduced in this book, and the publishers apologise for any inadvertent omissions.

The Lion, the Witch and the Wardrobe

SECTION 1

About the book

This fantasy-cum-allegory of Christ's passion, set in the Second World War, was first published in 1950 and rapidly became a modern classic of children's literature. It was followed by six more titles that together form *The Chronicles of Narnia*, named after the fictional country in which the adventures occur. Its characters range from talking animals to classical Greek and Norse mythology and even Father Christmas. The book has been dramatised for television and turned into a film. It is a fantasy adventure that stands in its own right, and may be used without reference to its religious parallels.

The story starts when a family of four wartime evacuees are sent away to escape the London air-raids. They arrive in a large historic house in the heart of the country, in the care of a kindly old professor.

They soon explore and, while investigating a large wardrobe, Lucy enters Narnia, where it is continual winter, but never Christmas. She meets a faun who befriends her, then admits his intention to give her up to the White Witch who put Narnia under its icy enchantment.

When Edmund later discovers Narnia, he meets the White Witch, who tempts him with empty promises. Back in the house, he denies having been there, upsetting truthful Lucy. At last, they all arrive in Narnia, where family loyalties are divided. So begins the good-versus-evil battle.

Aslan the lion arrives, to whom the children are introduced later by their new friends, the Beavers. Edmund, still trusting the Witch, betrays Aslan, but the lion's good magic is already thawing the frozen world. Edmund is about to be killed for disloyalty when Aslan's army intervenes and Aslan takes his place. Like Christ, he is tortured, humiliated and killed, but comes back to life. The White Witch is defeated in a battle fought, among others, by Peter and his reformed brother.

Peace is restored to Narnia, as Aslan brings petrified creatures back to life. The children become monarchs and rule long and wisely into adulthood. One day, they come across the way back into the wardrobe and return to their childhood lives at the very second at which they had left.

About the author

Clive Staples Lewis was born in Belfast in 1898 and died in 1963 (on the same day that President JF Kennedy was assassinated). He won a scholarship to Oxford in 1916 where his friends included JRR Tolkien, whose influence was a factor in Lewis becoming a Christian in 1931. Later, they both were members of a group calling themselves The Inklings, who met to discuss story plots and progress.

Facts and figures
Title: *The Lion, the Witch and the Wardrobe*
Author: C.S. Lewis
Original illustrator: Pauline Baynes
First published: 1950
Series: Part of *The Chronicles of Narnia*, a seven-book series. It is chronologically the second book, but was the first published. Television: adapted into a series first in 1976, and again in 1988.
Film: adapted in 2005 by Disney Pictures, followed by *Prince Caspian* in 2008 as part of *The Chronicles of Narnia* series.
Audio: one audio book, and three radio plays on CD.
Theatre: adapted in 1984, and staged at London's Westminster Theatre, and again in 1988 by the Royal Shakespeare Company among others.

Guided reading

SECTION 2

Before reading

Knowledge that *The Lion, the Witch and the Wardrobe* can be interpreted as an allegory of Christ's passion should not put off those who wish to read it purely at face value, as a fantasy adventure-cum-moral fable.

It is rare in a 20th-century children's book for an author to promote Christianity. However, in this book, the words of the famous Bible passage from Corinthians I are exemplified: *(Love is) patient, kind...never selfish*; and *...there are three things that last forever: faith, hope, and love; but the greatest of them all is love.* The values that the story promotes are common to all mainstream religions and to any humanistic set of moral principles. It offers scope for discussion regarding shared values and common ground between religions and non-believers' humane morality.

Meanwhile, the book, which begins in wartime Britain and was published soon after the end of the war, reflects many wartime experiences of hardship, loss, separation, tension and danger in a world of metaphorical winter and oppression.

Chapter 1: Lucy looks into a wardrobe

Peter, Susan, Edmund and Lucy arrive as wartime evacuees. Invite observations of how Edmund differs from his siblings, being argumentative and bad-tempered. Discuss how they list creatures they expect to see, learned by rote, not experience. Ask: *What shows the house is old and historic?* (A suit of armour, a harp and well-stocked library.)

Explain dated phrases: *mothballs* (to discourage moth larvae from nibbling holes); *wireless* (radio) and idioms such as *fallen on our feet* (been lucky) and *ten to one...* (there's a good chance...). Discuss why the author gives safety warnings about wardrobes. Such furniture would have had a catch or a key so they could only be opened from the outside.

When Lucy meets the faun, ask: *How does the author show that he is more human than animal?* (Through dress, manner, speech and actions.)

Chapter 2: What Lucy found there

Do the children recognise the source of *Daughter of Eve* as a synonym for a human female? Explain Adam and Eve: biblical names that represent the first humans on Earth.

Encourage the children to read aloud the word play of *Spare Oom* and *War Drobe*, comparing the real words. Ask: *What sorts of things remind you of fairy tales and myths?* (The stag who grants wishes; the winter enchantment; and references to mythical characters.)

Check children understand *under her thumb* (in her control). Ask the class for modern equivalents of Lucy's *Rather!* such as, *You bet!*

Chapter 3: Edmund and the wardrobe

Ask: *Why start a new chapter with the same dialogue as the previous chapter ended?* Suggest it urges readers to read on.

Edmund's behaviour is, again, at odds with that of his siblings. Ask: *How does it feel when people don't believe you?* Compare Lucy's hurt.

Explain *batty, goose* and *make it pax* meaning, respectively, 'mad', 'silly' and 'make friends'. Draw attention to use of the 'royal we' when the Queen says: *You shall know us better hereafter.* Ask: *What did Edmund think the Queen wanted to know when she asked* What are you? *that made him reply,* I'm at school*?* (He was probably thinking of trades and professions, such as, 'I am a butcher'.)

Chapter 4: Turkish Delight

Again the action and the conversation that close one chapter, open the next, encouraging reading stamina. Can the children work out the Queen's character from her condescending speech?

Ask: *What clues suggest the Queen is the witch?* Point out how, unlike Edmund, the reader knows Mr Tumnus' possible fate caused by indiscreet talk. Ask: *What, among the Queen's instructions should have warned Edmund that she was up to no good?* (Her insistence that he lie and deceive his family.) Explain *before*, meaning in front of.

Chapter 5: Back on this side of the door

This chapter deals with faith, trust and the nature of belief. Encourage the children to follow the Professor's logical approach to the older children's concern about Lucy's story. Note how he answers some questions with rhetorical questions.

Make sure the children understand the Professor's words: *quite at their disposal* (giving them his full attention). Invite the children to offer modern equivalents of *Sharp's the word*, such as *We're out of here!*

Chapter 6: Into the forest

Ask: *What does Susan's calling the housekeeper* the Macready *reveal about their opinion of her?* Explain how distancing adults' involvement enables the children to have their adventure unimpeded.

As all four children enter Narnia, invite readers to compare Peter's genuine apology to Lucy with Edmund's earlier non-apology. Ask: *What does their shaking hands indicate?* (Lucy forgives Peter.) Encourage them to observe Edmund's slyness, shown through his thoughts (inner dialogue) and his planting of doubt and fear in Peter's mind.

Chapter 7: A day with the Beavers

Invite the children to comment on the build-up of tension. Explain how the author reuses artefacts, carefully placed earlier: the lamppost, Lucy's handkerchief. Ask: *How does the handkerchief encourage the children to trust the beavers?*

Ask the children to consider the effect of Aslan's description. In turn, each character's feelings are described in an extended simile based within a dream-metaphor. Encourage the children to look closely at emotional responses to Aslan's name, considering what each reveals about them.

Explain that *before you could say Jack Robinson* means something instantaneous. Read the lists of the girls helping Mrs Beaver, long sentences creating a sense of busyness and readiness.

Chapter 8: What happened after dinner

Check the children understand *stratagem* (plan) and *pedlars* (sellers of wares). Ask: *What similes describe people's feelings on hearing Aslan's name?* Point out how the prophecies appear in rhyme.

Invite definitions of Mr Beaver's adjective applied to Edmund: *treacherous*. Compare Peter's exclamation *By Jove!* with modern equivalents.

Chapter 9: In the Witch's house

Half-jinn (genie), and half-giantess, the witch-queen represents evil, and is a temptress. Ask the children to note how the atmosphere builds up, combining Edmund's trepidation and bravado, mocking and desecrating the stone lion, while shaking with fear. Explain that, unlike the mythical creatures mentioned, *cat-a-mountain* is a romantic name for any wild mountain-cat, cougar or lynx. Discuss the closing cliff-hanger implication of a *harness without bells.*

Chapter 10: The spell begins to break

This chapter begins with the author's voice, reminding where Chapter 8 left off. (*And now of course...*) Invite children to observe the characters' solemn receiving of Father Christmas' presents. Ask: *How might these gifts serve as warnings?* (They imply imminent life-and-death battles.)

Chapter 11: Aslan is nearer

Draw attention to Lewis' use of understatement about Edmund's predicament: *...having a most disappointing time* and *...didn't look now as if the*

Witch intended to make him a King.

Examine how the gradual change is described, with the author's voice intervening to explain a jump in time. Note the pivotal change in Edmund as he shows sympathy for others.

Identify signs of a thaw, such as spring flowers and slushy snow. Focus on the onomatopoeic verbs describing the newly-flowing water.

Chapter 12: Peter's first battle

Ask: *How is the description broken up, unlike plain prose?* Clarify the difference between reported speech and direct speech. Ask: *What is similar about the* red rampant lion *(a standing lion) of Aslan's banner and the one on Peter's shield? What is* to velvet *a lion's paws?* (To retract claws.) Explain *win one's spurs*, as knights did, demonstrating their skills in battle.

Chapter 13: Deep Magic from the dawn of time

Contrast the names of the Witch's faithful with Aslan's. Ask: *How does the author show that Edmund is to be killed?* (His being tied up with his head pulled back, a knife being sharpened.) Note how he is aware only of sounds.

Aslan and the Witch come face to face to discuss the Deep Magic put into Narnia *at the very beginning by the Emperor-over-Sea*. Invite the children to compare the Witch's title *Empress of the Lone Islands*. Ask: *Who or what does Aslan's father's title remind you of?* (The Creator?) Despite knowing Edmund's life is safe, ask: *Why is there still concern?* (The Witch mentions a promise and has a look of 'fierce joy'.)

Chapter 14: The triumph of the Witch

This chapter is the moving account of Aslan's humiliating ridicule, torture and death. Ask: *How does the author show Aslan's sorrow?* (Through physical stance, deep sighs and distractedness.) His mood causes the girls' premonition that something dreadful is to happen.

Chapter 15: Deeper magic from before the dawn of time

Invite children to compare this chapter's title with that of Chapter 13. Ask: *Why are the words a cause of optimism?* (Perhaps the Witch has not won!) Point out how it is sound that reveals Aslan's resurrection. Discuss the emotional relief, to characters and readers, of the playful romp, that destroys hunger, thirst and tiredness. Point out the oxymoron: *soft roughness* and the prepositions that help detail their ride through Narnia: *over, across, down, through, past, up.*

Chapter 16: What happened about the statues

Explain that an extended simile (the paper's catching alight) is called an analogy. Highlight the focus on sounds (of animals). Explain *look alive* (hurry up). Ask: *What is Aslan quoting when he says* upstairs and downstairs and in my lady's chamber*?* (The nursery rhyme, Goosey goosey gander.) Note how Rumblebuffin offers comic relief after horror and sadness.

Chapter 17: The hunting of the white stag

Point out how Lucy's cordial comes into play at last (the author ties up ends and makes use of all artefacts introduced). Ask: *How well do the adjectives applied to the children suit them, when they are crowned?*

Discuss how the author changes the characters' style of speech as they grow older. What type of story does this reflect? Are they living in a fairy tale? Ask the children to think about how they might speak and feel when they get home.

Shared reading

SECTION 3

Extract 1

• Remind the children of the setting of this extract: Peter and Susan, having no experience as yet of Narnia, are concerned about Lucy's state of mind. They consider her more truthful than Edmund and yet they are finding her story hard to believe. This extract looks at the argument for trust, faith and the nature of belief, and may be compared with the nature of religious faith.

• Underline the question words how, why, what, and highlight how the Professor often answers questions with rhetorical questions of his own. Discuss the effect of this, forcing the child characters to rethink, or question their own reasoning.

• Ring words and phrases used to present possibilities, suppositions and hypotheses: *unless, assume, if, but, even if, likely, so, on the other hand,* and use of the conditional tense, *would have.*

• Draw attention to the function of the characters' conversation to pre-empt questions in the readers' minds, such as, *How come no time's passed?* Explain that even fantasy must have its own logic.

Extract 2

• Underline picturesque phrases that help build atmosphere: *...voice sank into silence* (compare 'stopped talking') and *mysterious nods.*

• Underline where the author's voice directly addresses the reader: *Perhaps it has sometimes happened to you...* Invite the children to look carefully at the detail in this extended simile. Ask the children how this is more effective than saying simply, *it was like an amazingly significant and memorable dream.* (The author takes the reader through each stage of the dream and its aftermath analogy – revealing how the variants of the dream will affect the dreamer's response.)

• Highlight each child character's emotional response, underlining their names and the verb *felt.* Ring the adjectives that describe them: *mysterious, brave, adventurous, delicious, delightful.* Draw attention to the absence of adjectives in the description of Lucy's reaction: it is another short analogy.

• Remind the children of the five senses: touch, taste, sight, smell, and hearing. Write in the margin any senses that are stimulated throughout the extract, beginning with sound or its absence (*silence,* then *a low whisper*); vision (nods and beckoning); touch (tickling whiskers and a 'butterflies inside' type of feeling); mentions of smell; and then sound (music) once again.

Extract 3

• This extract also begins with an analogy. Explain that it is a comparison between one thing and another to explain something. Discuss how this analogy indicates the era in which the story was written, when most houses had grates and open fires, pre-central heating.

• Underline words that may need more explanation: *marble* (a valuable stone and very cold to the touch: in contrast to the flame analogy); *hindquarters* (its back end and back legs); *rippled* (invite the children to move their fingers in a quick, wavy motion); *prodigious* (enormous, amazing); *frisked* (gambolled); *whimpering* (giving feeble cries).

• Invite children to compare the contrasting atmosphere of a museum and a zoo. Compare, too, the white snow-covered landscape and grey stone figures with the dazzlingly bright array of sudden colour; the stillness and the frenzy.

• Highlight the colour adjectives and underline the names of the tree-girls or woodland nymphs. Explain these are referred to elsewhere as *dryads.*

Extract 1

From Chapter 5: Back on this side of the door

"You know she doesn't tell lies and it is obvious that she is not mad. For the moment then and unless any further evidence turns up, we must assume that she is telling the truth."

Susan looked at him very hard and was quite sure from the expression on his face that he was not making fun of them.

"But how could it be true, sir?" said Peter.

"Why do you say that?" asked the Professor.

"Well, for one thing," said Peter, "if it was real why doesn't everyone find this country every time they go to the wardrobe? I mean, there was nothing there when we looked; even Lucy didn't pretend there was."

"What has that to do with it?" said the Professor.

"Well, sir, if things are real, they're there all the time."

"Are they?" said the Professor; and Peter did not know quite what to say.

"But there was no time," said Susan. "Lucy had had no time to have gone anywhere, even if there was such a place. She came running after us the very moment we were out of the room. It was less than a minute, and she pretended to have been away for hours."

"That is the very thing that makes her story so likely to be true," said the Professor. "If there really is a door in this house that leads to some other world (and I should warn you that this is a very strange house, and even I know very little about it) – if, I say, she had got into another world, I should not be at all surprised to find that the other world had a separate time of its own; so that however long you stayed there it would never take up any of our time. On the other hand, I don't think many girls of her age would invent that idea for themselves. If she had been pretending, she would have hidden for a reasonable time before coming out and telling her story."

Extract 2

From Chapter 7: A day with the Beavers

Here the Beaver's voice sank into silence and it gave one or two very mysterious nods. Then signalling to the children to stand as close around it as they possibly could, so that their faces were actually tickled by its whiskers, it added in a low whisper –

"They say Aslan is on the move – perhaps has already landed."

And now a very curious thing happened. None of the children knew who Aslan was any more than you do; but the moment the Beaver had spoken these words everyone felt quite different. Perhaps it has sometimes happened to you in a dream that someone says something which you don't understand but in the dream it feels as if it has some enormous meaning – either a terrifying one which turns the whole dream into a nightmare or else a lovely meaning too lovely to put into words, which makes the dream so beautiful that you remember it all your life and are always wishing you could get into that dream again. It was like that now. At the name of Aslan each one of the children felt something jump in its inside. Edmund felt a sensation of mysterious horror. Peter felt suddenly brave and adventurous. Susan felt as if some delicious smell or some delightful strain of music had just floated by her. And Lucy got the feeling you have when you wake up in the morning and realise that is the beginning of the holidays or the beginning of summer.

Extract 3

From Chapter 16: What happened about the statues

I expect you've seen someone put a lighted match to a bit of newspaper which is propped up in a grate against an unlit fire. And for a second nothing seems to have happened; and then you notice a tiny streak of flame creeping along the edge of the newspaper. It was like that now. For a second after Aslan had breathed upon him the stone lion looked just the same. Then a tiny streak of gold began to run along his white marble back – then it spread – then the colour seemed to lick all over him as the flame licks all over the bit of paper – then, while his hindquarters were still obviously stone, the lion shook his mane and all the heavy, stony folds rippled into living hair. Then he opened a great red mouth, warm and living, and gave a prodigious yawn. And now his hind legs had come to life. He lifted one of them and scratched himself. Then, having caught sight of Aslan, he went bounding after him and frisking round him whimpering with delight and jumping up to lick his face.

Of course the children's eyes turned to follow the lion; but the sight they saw was so wonderful that they soon forgot about *him.* Everywhere the statues were coming to life. The courtyard looked no longer like a museum; it looked more like a zoo. Creatures were running after Aslan and dancing round him till he was almost hidden in the crowd. Instead of all that deadly white the courtyard was now a blaze of colours; glossy chestnut sides of centaurs, indigo horns of unicorns, dazzling plumage of birds, reddy-brown of foxes, dogs and satyrs, yellow stockings and crimson hoods of dwarfs; and the birch-girls in silver, and the beech-girls in fresh, transparent green, and the larch-girls in green so bright that it was almost yellow.

Plot, character and setting

SECTION 4

Fairy-tale features

Objective: To infer writer's perspective from what is written and from what is implied.
What you need: Copies of *The Lion, the Witch and the Wardrobe* and writing materials.

What to do

- Read the dedication aloud to the class and list what they expect to find in a fairy tale: traditional phrases (such as *Once upon a time…*, *happily ever after*; stereotypical characters (heroes, villains); magic wishes, spells or powers; special tasks; obstacles; and a faraway land, akin to ours, yet different.
- Ask the children to read Chapter 1 and note fairy-tale components, from language style to content.
- Invite them to share their findings. These might include the opening words *Once there were…*; the magical entry into a different world; a strange person.
- Discuss how this chapter differs from a traditional fairy tale: more detail, opening with a real situation and moving into fantasy, deeper character development. Compare with a classic fairy tale, for example, 'Jack was lazy'.
- Do the children notice that it is the faun who is startled at the sight of Lucy, not the reverse? What might the author wish to suggest by this? (If he is shocked, she is a startling sight and unexpected.)

Differentiation
For older/more confident learners: Encourage the children to read Chapter 2, listing further fairy-tale references: the stag that grants wishes, the winter enchantment and mythical gods.
For younger/less confident learners: Give each child, with a reading partner, a list of fairy-tale elements to look out for as they read, and ask them to identify and make a note of them. Spread the reading over more than one session.

Why there? Why them? Why then?

Objective: To understand underlying themes, causes and points of view.
What you need: Copies of *The Lion, the Witch and the Wardrobe*, Extract 1 on page 8, photocopiable page 15 and writing materials.
Cross-curricular links: History, PSHE.

What to do

- Explain that *The Lion, the Witch and the Wardrobe* was published at a time of post-war optimism. If your class has not studied the Second World War, then briefly discuss it.
- Ask: *How does this influence the author's choice of characters, setting and plot?* (It offers a message of hope, after six years' war – compare the continual winter and arrival of spring; and an end to war – the arrival of Aslan to overpower the Witch.) *What is achieved by removing the children from their home?* (More freedom.)
- Discuss the Professor's role. Why is he necessary to the plot? (To add plausibility and reassurance that a grown-up knows where the characters are and what they are doing, providing a role model of responsibility, *in loco parentis*.)
- Read Extract 1 together. Talk about the Professor's logical reasoning. Draw attention to his answering questions with rhetorical ones. Discuss why they found his response surprising.
- Hand out copies of the photocopiable page 15 for the children to complete.

Differentiation
For older/more confident learners: Challenge the children to comment on the misfit character of Edmund and his role in the story.
For younger/less confident learners: Prepare word cards to prompt recognition of symbols and similarities between Narnia at the beginning of the book, and a world war.

Plot, character and setting

SECTION 4

Sensational narrative

Objective: To compare the usefulness of techniques such as visualisation, prediction and empathy in exploring the meaning of texts.
What you need: Copies of *The Lion, the Witch and the Wardrobe*, Extract 2 on page 9, photocopiable page 16 and writing materials.

What to do

- After you have read Chapter 7, talk about Mr Beaver's first (silent) communication: *the animal put its paw against its mouth…* Discuss how personification and simile help readers to picture the scene and empathise.
- Read Extract 2 up to the end of the first direct speech. Ask: *Does this sentence indicate who or what Aslan is?* Discuss what *landed* might suggest. (A flying creature?) *What might* on the move *suggest?*
- Finish reading the extract. Ask the children to note how the author involves the five senses. Underline: *mysterious nods* (sight); *tickled by its whiskers* (touch); *a low whisper* and *strain of music* (sound); *delicious smell* (scent). Can the children find other examples (including taste)?
- Discuss the characters' reactions to Aslan's name. Ask: *What do these reveal about the children as much as Aslan?*
- Ask the children to complete photocopiable page 16.

Differentiation
For older/more confident learners: Ask the children if hearing any name or word has a strong effect on them. Encourage them to write a paragraph explaining how and, if possible, why they react strongly or explain their reaction to a partner.
For younger/less confident learners: Provide dictionaries for the children to look up the meanings of unfamiliar words on the photocopiable sheet.

Parallel events

Objective: To understand how authors use different structures to create coherence and impact.
What you need: Copies of *The Lion, the Witch and the Wardrobe*, plain A4 paper, writing materials, photocopiable page 17 and scissors.
Cross-curricular link: History.

What to do

- Write each opening sentence of Chapters 9 and 10, and indicate how the author's voice explains the switch between scenes.
- Ask: *Why would this device be more necessary in 1950 than today?* (Few families had television then; children now are used to seeing scene-switches between simultaneous events in soaps, films and dramas.) Can the children supply a single word that serves the purpose of switching to a parallel scene in narrative? (Meanwhile.)
- Talk about why, when Edmund is shaking with fear, he is able to mock Aslan and desecrate the stone lion. Explain how this boosts his courage and is called 'bravado': a kind of mock-bravery.
- Discuss why the author distances the modern image of Father Christmas from the Narnia character, an equally bountiful, but more solemn version, whose gifts match his seriousness.
- Ask the children to fold a sheet of A4 paper horizontally and label the upper half Chapter 9, and the lower half Chapter 10. Ask them to make brief notes in the present tense to create, in parallel sequence, a timeline of events.

Differentiation
For older/more confident learners: Create a brief glossary of some of the themes (good, evil, altar, temptation, boy, girl). See if the children can match them to Aslan, the White Witch, the Stone Table Turkish Delight, Adam's son and Eve's daughter.
For younger/less confident learners: Hand out photocopiable page 17 and scissors, for the children to cut out the cue cards for respective chapters to sequence and expand into notes.

Plot, character and setting

SECTION 4

Ways with words

Objective: To explore how word meanings change when used in different contexts.
What you need: Copies of *The Lion, the Witch and the Wardrobe,* individual whiteboards and pens, and individual writing materials.

What to do

- Write these words on the board for the children to copy on to their individual whiteboards as a vertical list: *creature, grinned, fast, delicious, chuckle, pretty, rich, velvet, mouth, stroke.*
- Allow them five minutes to write a short definition or synonym alongside each word.
- Invite the children to share and embellish their responses by asking questions, such as: *What emotion is suggested by* grinned? *Give an example of a* creature. *Name something* delicious.
- Hand out copies of the book and ask the children to scan Chapters 11 and 12 and find these words in context. (They appear in order.)
- As each is found, invite comments on how the meaning or use of the word compares. For example, draw attention to the phrase modifying how the dwarf grinned (*in a repulsive manner*); Why is Edmund referred to as a *creature*?
- Encourage the children to recognise how context affects meaning: some words have different meanings (such as *fast*), while others are used in a figurative way, such as *delicious* – of visual sunlight; then of the sounds of water and birdsong.

Differentiation
For older/more confident learners: Ask the children to add variant definitions alongside their original notes, marking 'n' for noun, 'a' for adjective and so on.
For younger/less confident learners: Use sticky notes in the margin of the text to highlight the words' appearance and so help the children to locate them.

Good, bad or a bit of both?

Objective: To make notes on and use evidence from across a text to explain events or ideas.
What you need: Copies of *The Lion, the Witch and the Wardrobe,* Extract 2 on page 9, photocopiable page 18, writing materials.
Cross-curricular link: PSHE.

What to do

- Invite the class to talk about the children's characters in the story. Display Extract 2 and underline the sentences that show how each character felt on hearing Aslan's name.
- Discuss the feeling of 'butterflies in the stomach' and what events and emotions cause this feeling: fear, excitement, anticipation and shock. Invite brief anecdotes from individuals .
- Ask the children which character had a negative feeling. Discuss how you can inexplicably 'feel inside' that something is going wrong or is threatening your peace of mind.
- Ask the children to offer further examples where Edmund's behaviour or reaction has differed markedly from his siblings'.
- Hand out photocopiable page 18 and ask the children to refer to the book to answer the questions. Explain that no one is all good or all bad. Encourage them to consider how Edmund changes and redeems himself. Discuss the distinction between doing a bad thing and being bad.
- Bring the class together to discuss their findings and gain a consensus about the character.

Differentiation
For older/more confident learners: Invite children to write a paragraph on each of the other child characters.
For younger/less confident learners: Ask the children to discuss with a partner whether they would like Edmund as a friend or brother and explain why. Share their opinions and reasons with the rest of the class.

Analogies and contrasts

Objective: To explore how writers use language for comic and dramatic effect.
What you need: Copies of *The Lion, the Witch and the Wardrobe*, Extract 3 on page 10, different coloured highlighters, Extract 2 on page 9 and writing materials.
Cross-curricular link: History.

What to do

- Read Extract 3 together. Ask: *How many of you have a grate at home? What does this first paragraph suggest about the era in which the book was written?* (It predates central heating, when open fires were the norm.)
- Explain that an extended simile is called an analogy. The author chose something in his readers' experience, so they could picture it.
- Ask: *What aspects of starting a fire are similar to life returning to the stone lion?* (Nothing seems to happen at first, then gradually fire/colour spreads until, suddenly, it 'comes to life'.)
- Invite the children to compare the first paragraph with the second, which emphasises the contrast between a white, frozen world and sudden colour, bustle and life.
- In different colours, highlight each colour adjective, and each motion verb.
- Challenge children to create an analogy to describe a feeling, such as relief. (*It's like walking into a hot kitchen after building a snowman.*)

Differentiation
For older/more confident learners: Challenge children to extend and embellish their analogy, such as adding, *You know how you feel as if you have six toes in each boot and you can't stop shivering, and then...*
For younger/less confident learners: Provide Extract 2, which contains another analogy from Chapter 7. Can they identify which part is the analogy? (The description of a dream.)

Thence to now!

Objective: To compare different types of narrative and information texts and identify how they are structured.
What you need: Copies of *The Lion, the Witch and the Wardrobe* and a whiteboard.

What to do

- Write the titles that the children gain in the final chapter on the board: *Peter the Magnificent, Susan the Gentle, Edmund the Just* and *Lucy the Valiant.* Discuss how well their titles suit them. Ensure children understand the meaning of *just* (invite comparison with the noun 'justice') and *valiant* (brave).
- Discuss which title shows the biggest contrast to the beginning of the story (Edmund's).
- Read aloud from the final chapter where, having been kings and queens for so long, the children have begun to speak differently. Apart from humour, what effect does this stylised conversation have? Are they 'living the fairy tale'?
- Read aloud, from *Then said King Peter...* ask one child to act as narrator and four others to read the direct speech in character.
- Talk about how this narrative differs from the rest. Ask the children to note how suddenly the style changes, before any character speaks, by reversing the word order from *Peter then said* and adding his title, *King.*
- Challenge them to translate phrases into a modern language.

Differentiation
For older/more confident learners: Invite the children to create a glossary of phrases to accompany Chapter 17.
For younger/less confident learners: Prompt the children by offering comparisons such as *tree of iron: we wouldn't say a chair of wood, we'd say a wooden chair, so...* Mime an action, such as 'set it here' to encourage the children to offer 'put it here'.

Why there? Why them? Why then?

- Think about similarities between life in wartime Britain and life in Narnia in *The Lion, the Witch and the Wardrobe.* For example:

> A war that begins when a dictator tries to rule over all of Europe is like what happens when an evil witch casts a powerful spell over Narnia, making it winter all year round.

- Here are more things that happen in wartime. Below each, write what or who is similar, and how, in *The Lion, the Witch and the Wardrobe.*

People living side by side but divided into friends and enemies is like…

___

Some people working 'underground' to help and protect friends and plot against the enemy is like…

___

Spies listening to secret plans and then passing them on to the enemy is like…

___

Some people, who pretend to be a friend when all the time they are working for the enemy, are like…

___

Getting rid of the Witch, unfreezing stone statues, and enjoying the return of spring to Narnia, is like…

___

Glossary

dictator – a ruler with total power over a country
invasion – taking over, seizing power
the underground – a group which works in secret against an existing power
air raid – an attack by aircraft dropping bombs on to a target
evacuee – a person sent away from a place of danger

Sensational narrative

- Read the feelings in the boxes below. Which best describe which child, based on their reactions to the name of Aslan?
- Write the character's name and a quotation from the extract to support your opinion.
- Use a dictionary to help you.

excitement and happy anticipation

Child ______________________

Quotation ______________________

____

confusion, dread and trepidation

Child ______________________

Quotation ______________________

____

peace and contentment

Child ______________________

Quotation ______________________

____

gallantry, curiosity and responsibility

Child ______________________

Quotation ______________________

____

SCHOLASTIC
www.scholastic.co.uk

Parallel events

- Cut out the cards and order each set of events as they occur in Chapters 9 and 10 of *The Lion, the Witch and the Wardrobe.*
- Use the cards to write notes to create a parallel timeline for Edmund's actions and his brother's and sisters' actions.

Chapter 9	Chapter 10
Edmund overhears Mr Beaver	Father Christmas arrives with gifts
White Witch's house	urgent preparations
slips out alone	have breakfast before setting off
courtyard – stone figures	snowing and icy
moonlight	Beavers and children sleep
Wolf – Maugrim	enter underground hiding place
Queen orders sleigh with no bells	they all grow impatient to leave
tells Queen the plan	Stone Table

Good, bad or a bit of both?

- Answer these questions about Edmund's behaviour at different points in the story of *The Lion, the Witch and the Wardrobe.*

1. How does Edmund behave when he first meets the Professor?

2. How does he react when Lucy tells the others about the magic wardrobe?

3. What does Edmund tell the Witch about his brothers and sisters?

4. How does he let Lucy down after his first visit to Narnia?

5. What are Edmund's main reasons for wanting to return to Narnia?

6. What does he do after the Beavers have explained when and where Aslan plans to meet the children?

7. How does Edmund react over the stone figures in the queen's courtyard?

8. What does he do when he sees the Witch raise her wand over the Christmas dinner party?

9. What is the first thing Edmund does when he is reunited with the others?

10. How does Edmund behave during the battle with the Witch?

- Use your answers to help you to describe Edmund's character. On another sheet, explain how and when he begins to change.

Talk about it

SECTION 5

Mythical creatures

Objective: To devise a performance considering how to adapt the performance for a specific audience.
What you need: Copies of *The Lion, the Witch and the Wardrobe*, photocopiable page 22 and children's reference books describing mythical creatures and Greek gods.
Cross-curricular link: Drama.

What to do

- Explain that *The Lion, the Witch and the Wardrobe* combines reality and fantasy with characters from classical mythology.
- Ask: *Which mythical creature appears in Chapter 1?* Invite descriptions of the faun's appearance.
- Hand out the photocopiable sheet to groups of five or six. Allow them time to read the glossary and research further details of the creatures, adding to the notes provided.
- Explain that you want each group to plan a short performance to introduce some of the creatures. They must decide who their audience is – parents, younger children or a mixed audience. They must also choose and improvise (or roughly script) a scenario to introduce the characters.
- Suggest ideas and invite more, such as a spoof catwalk parade (for example, 'This year the faun-about-forest is sporting short curly horns, wearing his beard short, and carrying his tail. No faun will be seen out in anything other than high hoofs', and so on) or a party where the audience can 'eavesdrop' on mythical party-goers introducing themselves to one another.
- Allow time for the children to prepare and perform their act. Suggest that the actors mime their part(s) and, if required, one child acts as narrator.

Differentiation
For older/more confident learners: Spread the activity over more than one session, allowing time for each group to prepare props and make masks or minimal costumes.
For younger/less confident learners: Nominate one or two characters for each respective group to research. Ask each group to provide one or two actors to take lead-roles in a whole-class performance in a prearranged format. All the class can be involved as 'extras'.

Christian allegory

Objective: To infer writer's perspective from what is written and from what is implied.
What you need: Copies of *The Lion, the Witch and the Wardrobe*, photocopiable page 23 and writing materials.
Cross-curricular link: PSHE.

What to do

- Read the dedication from the book and explain the role of godfather. Discuss what it means to have faith or believe in something. Ask: *How is faith different from certain knowledge?*
- Explain to the children that some people have no faith. Ask: *Is it possible for non-religious people to practise a kind of faith on a daily basis?*
- Explain that a book whose narrative is symbolic of another is an allegory, almost like the same story 'in disguise'.
- Divide the class into groups and hand out copies of the book and photocopiable page 23. Ask each group to discuss what aspects of the story can be seen as allegorical.

Differentiation
For older/more confident learners: Challenge individual children to write a paragraph to explain in what ways Aslan is like Jesus Christ.
For younger/less confident learners: Write brief cue cards to help the children to recognise allegorical events: *Edmund and Turkish Delight; Peter goes into battle; Aslan agrees to be killed in place of Edmund; Aslan is bound, shaved and humiliated; Aslan's resurrection; forgiveness of Edmund.*

Talk about it

SECTION 5

From script to stage

Objective: To perform a scripted scene making use of dramatic conventions
What you need: Copies of *The Lion, the Witch and the Wardrobe* and Extract 1 on page 8.
Cross-curricular link: Drama.

What to do

- Point out that there are many dramatic moments in *The Lion, the Witch and the Wardrobe.* Some are quietly dramatic, such as Mr Tumnus' sudden change of heart and Aslan's sad preparation for his ordeal, to more active drama, such as the Beavers' preparations for their journey with the children.
- Ask the children to find a partner and choose which scene they would like to dramatise. Advise them to pick a scene that includes dialogue and, if possible, a variety of mood, voice, different levels of tension, and so on.
- Together, they should create a script for themselves and up to two others. They could type parts, using different coloured fonts for different characters. They should also add simple stage directions and any props required.
- Explain that you are looking for accurate scripting (loyal to the original text) and quality of delivery of the lines, in terms of pace, volume, tone and expression, and physically adopting each role, rather than duration.

Differentiation
For older/more confident learners: Ask the children to add a short spoken introduction, to set the scene in context.
For younger/less confident learners: Provide Extract 1 and ask each child, in groups of three, to highlight the respective speeches of the Professor, Susan and Peter. Stage directions can be underlined.

Do you remember?

Objective: To reflect on how working in role helps to explore complex issues.
What you need: Copies of *The Lion, the Witch and the Wardrobe,* Extract 2 on page 9 and photocopiable page 24.
Cross-curricular link: Drama.

What to do

- Explain that the children are going to plan and present a radio-style broadcast of two characters.
- Explain that the author consistently shows the characters' complex feelings, sometimes specifically (underline the statements in Extract 2), and sometimes by showing their behaviour. Ask: *How did Lucy feel when Mr Tumnus couldn't stop crying? How did Peter feel when Aslan was giving him advice on how to conduct the forthcoming battle?*
- Ask the children to work with a partner and to choose two of the child characters. Ask them to imagine that their characters are now grown up. Explain that they must plan a conversation between their characters, where they reminisce about their adventure, concentrating on their feelings at the time.
- Give each child photocopiable page 24 on which they can make notes to help extemporise their conversation.
- Listen to the children's conversations. Invite listeners to compare their own in-role feelings. Discuss how far working in role increases empathy with characters.

Differentiation
For older/more confident learners: Allow the children to experiment holding a four-way conversation between all four main characters.
For younger/less confident learners: Prompt the children with questions to elicit responses, such as, *Susan, how did you feel when the Professor claimed that Lucy could be telling the truth?*

Talk about it

SECTION 5

Believe me!

Objective: To analyse the use of persuasive language.
What you need: Copies of *The Lion, the Witch and the Wardrobe* and writing materials.
Cross-curricular link: PSHE.

What to do

- Ask the children to read the last sentences of Chapter 1 and those opening Chapter 2. Ask them to note how Lucy begins with words of reassurance that she is 'back' unharmed.
- Challenge the children to find other things she says, and the way she words them, that suggest she is trying to persuade the others to believe her. For example, she opens a sentence with *But...* implying that they have to believe her if she tells her story logically; expressions such as *really and truly, honestly* and, finally, being lost for words and bursting into tears of frustration.
- Ask the children, individually or in pairs, to think of something, true or invented, which others might have difficulty believing. Explain that they must make notes on what credibility-stretching experience they will describe, how they will make it sound plausible, and how they will react if they cannot convince others.
- Listen to some performances and invite comments on the use of persuasive language.

Differentiation
For older/more confident learners: Pair narrators with an opponent who ridicules their story and offers contradictory 'evidence' so that the speakers have to think quickly to defend their stories.
For younger/less confident learners: Present a choice of scenarios for the children to choose from, such as arriving at school early to find a monkey in the classroom and suchlike.

From tableau to action

Objective: To sustain engagement with longer texts, using techniques to make the text come alive.
What you need: Copies of *The Lion, the Witch and the Wardrobe* and Extract 3 on page 10.

Cross-curricular link: Drama.

What to do

- Read Extract 3 together. Ask the children to note how still and silent the scene is at the onset, and how gradually all the petrified creatures come back to life as Aslan breathes on them.
- Divide them into groups of six to eight. Invite them to locate the extract in Chapter 16 and have one child in each group list the sounds: *roarings, cooings, brayings*, and so on. Ask them also to list the statues, including the lion and the faun.
- Nominate one child in each group to act the part of Aslan. The others must choose a character and an appropriate cry. Discuss, for example, which mythical creatures might bray or neigh.
- Challenge each group to plan a performance of the scene. They must begin with a tableau, playing the parts of still statues in the courtyard. They must decide who Aslan will bring to life first, and how each creature will react: scratching? stretching? rubbing eyes? They should gradually build their performance to a crescendo of happy cries and dancing.
- Explain how to choreograph their performance – deciding broadly on how each initial stance will vary and how to coordinate their movements.

Differentiation
For older/more confident learners: Encourage the children to extend the scene to incorporate direct dialogue from the book, such as Aslan's, the other lion's and Giant Rumblebuffin's.
For younger/less confident learners: Encourage the children to draw a simple 2D plan of where they will stand at the beginning – such as four corners of a square with the lion in the centre. They could make chalk marks on the floor to mark their positions.

Mythical creatures

- Here are brief descriptions of mythical creatures that appear in *The Lion, the Witch and the Wardrobe*. You may like to add more details.

faun	woodland creature, half-man, half-goat, with short curly horns and beard, hairy legs, hoofs and long tail
satyr	similar to a faun, but larger, usually with a goat's tail
centaur	half-man, half-horse, from ancient Greek mythology
dryads	tree women, such as larch-girls, beech-girls and birch-girls; woodland nymphs
naiads	well-women or other water nymphs
Bacchus and Silenus	Greek gods of wine and intoxication
ogre	man-eating giant
ghoul	ghost or spirit preying on corpses, from Eastern tales
Minotaur	Greek mythical beast: half-man, half-bull, the upper half having arms, body and head of a man
spectre	shadowy ghost or spirit representing especially war, ruin, famine or madness
boggle	kind of boggart or evil goblin-like spirit
hag	ugly witch or old female evil spirit

Christian allegory

• *The Lion, the Witch and the Wardrobe* has been called an allegory of the life of Jesus Christ and of believers who have done wrong but, being sorry, are saved through Jesus' self-sacrifice when he was put to death on the cross. (Explain that an allegory is a story, poem, or picture which can be seen to have a hidden meaning.)

• Read these statements about Christian beliefs and the story of Jesus Christ's earthly life, death and resurrection (his coming back to life). Which part of C.S. Lewis' story symbolises each of these aspects of Christian tradition?

1. Sometimes people are tempted by bad things, which lead away from God.

____

2. Belief requires trust and faith. Sometimes what seems impossible is true.

____

3. Christians should fight against evil and call on Jesus Christ to help them.

____

4. Jesus gave his life for sinners so that, if they believe in him and repent of their sins, their lives can be saved.

____

5. Before Jesus was put to death on the cross, his persecutors taunted and mocked him, tying him up, putting a 'crown' of painful thorns on his head, taking away his valuable seamless coat and holding a lottery to win it.

____

6. Three days after Jesus was put to death, he rose back to life.

____

7. Jesus told Christians to be kind, compassionate and forgiving to others.

____

Do you remember?

- Ring the character whose role you are going to adopt.

Peter	Susan	Edmund	Lucy

- How does your chosen character feel…

1. …when they arrive at the Professor's house?

2. …when they reach Narnia?

3. …when they all follow the robin and meet the Beavers?

4. …when they meet another major character (choose one of the following): Mr Tumnus/Aslan/the White Witch?

5. …on seeing Aslan (choose one of the following): killed/found alive again/ preparing for battle?

6. …on becoming a king or a queen?

7. …when they arrive back in the house at the same moment that they left?

Prophetic poems

Objective: To adapt non-narrative form and styles to write fiction or factual texts, including poems.
What you need: Copies of *The Lion, the Witch and the Wardrobe* and writing materials.
Cross-curricular link: PSHE.

What to do

- Invite the children to share folklore rhymes that predict the weather, such as 'Red sky at night: shepherds' delight...' or 'Oak (in leaf) before ash: in for a splash; Ash before oak: in for a soak' or 'May wet and windy: barn full and plenty'. Explain that these are ancient bits of wisdom and how rhyme makes them memorable; appealing to children from generation to generation. Explain that a prophesy predicts the future.
- Read aloud the prophetic verses in Chapter 8. Of the first, ask the children: *What is wrong in Narnia?* (Always winter, never Christmas; people in fear of being turned to stone.) Which season equates to *wrong* and *sorrow* and which to *right*?
- Of the second verse, ask: *What is meant by 'Adam's flesh' and 'Adam's bone'? Can you predict who might occupy the thrones at Cair Paravel?*
- Ask the children, individually, to think what could change in the future or what they would like to see changed. This could be something serious: a water shortage, or frivolous: an era of no homework. Ask them to write a short rhyming, rhythmic verse expressing the prediction.

Differentiation
For older/more confident learners: Challenge the children to write a short story based on, and containing, their verse.
For younger/less confident learners: Allow children to work with a partner. Suggest useful rhymes that link with their chosen subject – such as (water shortage): thirst, worst, burst, cursed, first, nursed.

In my own words

Objective: To reflect independently and critically on their own writing and edit and improve it.
What you need: Copies of *The Lion, the Witch and the Wardrobe*, Extract 3 on page 10 and writing materials.
Cross-curricular link: Drama.

What to do

- Read Extract 3 together, and highlight each word relating to life or death: *breathed, living hair, red mouth, warm and living; a museum, deadly white.* Discuss the images that the word *museum* conjures up.
- Underline where the author's voice begins the extract: *I expect you've seen*, speaking directly to the reader, and inviting empathy. Note how the next paragraph invites the reader to look through the characters' eyes, as they 'turned to follow the lion'. (They are outside the scene, looking on.)
- Challenge the children to imagine themselves inside the scene. Ask them to imagine being the lion as he comes back to life. Can they perform a *prodigious* (amazing, enormous) *yawn*?
- Invite the children to find the extract in Chapter 16 and read more about the lion's reactions.
- Provide writing materials and ask the children to retell the scene, in the first person, as the lion, embellishing the detail from their imagination.
- Invite the children to read their work aloud, and redraft any sections that can be improved.

Differentiation
For older/more confident learners: Invite children to write in the first person, adopting the persona of Mr Tumnus, or one of the other stone characters.
For younger/less confident learners: Ask children to rewrite lines from the original text, translating them into the first person, but remembering that they cannot see themselves as an onlooker can – they can only feel, hear, and so on. For example: 'I felt a hot streak begin to run along my marble back.'

Get writing

SECTION 6

By Jove, it's dated!

Objective: To compare how writers from different times and places present experiences and use language.
What you need: Copies of *The Lion, the Witch and the Wardrobe*, photocopiable page 28 and writing materials.
Cross-curricular links: History, PSHE.

What to do

- Suggest that *The Lion, the Witch and the Wardrobe*, although set in 1940s wartime Britain, and published in 1950, is a timeless story and could take place anywhere. The story is as relevant and enjoyable today as it was when it was first written. Indeed, in 2005, a major film adaptation of the book filled cinema seats.
- What aspects of the narrative sound 'dated' – of their era, and therefore, old-fashioned? Note that the repeated advice never to shut oneself in a wardrobe predates 'health and safety' laws. Point out, too, how modern fitted wardrobes can be opened from the inside. Ask: *How many of you have a cotton handkerchief in your pocket? Who has a tissue?* This important item, used as a token of good faith by Mr Beaver, was common then.
- Establish that the children's spoken language, especially informal phrases, date the book.
- Hand out photocopiable page 28 and ask the children to write modern translations of the dated phrases to create a glossary.

Differentiation
For older/more confident learners: Ask them to imagine writing a story set in the future. Challenge them to invent futuristic-sounding phrases to replace those in the double-era glossary.
For younger/less confident learners: Challenge the children to research and compile a list of exclamations, old and new: how many can they find?

Adapting true stories

Objective: To experiment with different narrative form and styles to write their own stories.
What you need: Copies of *The Lion, the Witch and the Wardrobe*, photocopiable page 29 and writing materials.
Cross-curricular links: History, PSHE.

What to do

- Discuss how *The Lion, the Witch and the Wardrobe* can be viewed as an allegory of the life of Christ, Aslan representing Jesus, rising from the dead and saving humans from earthly evil and their own wrong-doing. Explain that an allegory is similar to a parody, except that it usually deals with serious subject matter.
- Challenge the children to take a famous, true story and plan their own story that is an allegory. For example, they might look at Captain Scott's attempt to be first to reach the South Pole or Helen Keller's battle with blindness and deafness to learn sign language and be able to lead an independent life and help others.
- Explain that their main character will be based on the main character in the true story. Explain that an anthropomorphised animal has human characteristics. Suggest that they may use some or all anthropomorphised animal characters. Point out how animals should match the characters, such as the lion – noble, strong 'king of the jungle'; beavers – industrious, strong, resourceful; mice – numerous and with sharp teeth; and robin – friendly and tame.
- Hand out copies of photocopiable page 29 to help children's planning.

Differentiation:
For older/more confident learners: Challenge the children to write their stories in short, titled chapters.
For younger/less confident learners: Provide a selection of true stories for the children to read and refresh their memories of characters and events.

Get writing

SECTION 6

Narrative techniques

Objective: To use different narrative techniques to engage and entertain the reader.
What you need: Copies of *The Lion, the Witch and the Wardrobe*, Extract 2 on page 9 and writing materials.

What to do

- Ask the children to help you list different narrative techniques used in *The Lion, the Witch and the Wardrobe*: straight description, use of simile and analogy, direct speech, reported speech, poems, comic interludes, change of direct-speech style in the final chapter to a humorously cumbersome, archaic, pretentious style.
- Quote examples of how the author speaks to the reader, such as *I hope you know what I mean by a voice sounding pale* (Chapter 10); *I hope no one who reads this book has ever been quite as miserable as Susan and Lucy were that night* (Chapter 15).

Read the dream section of Extract 2.

- Allow the children five minutes to draft some opening sentences that address the reader with a rhetorical question, such as *Have you ever had a dream where you are in a strange building, yet know your way around?*
- Listen to some examples, and then ask each child to choose one as a springboard for an adventure story.
- Challenge them to involve a variety of writing styles in writing their stories.

Differentiation
For older/more confident learners: Challenge the children to expand the rhetorical questions into a longer analogy at the opening of their stories.
For younger/less confident learners: Take one of the two suggestions above and develop a plot and structure as a whole-class activity, before children write the stories individually.

What do you believe in?

Objective: To express subtle distinctions of meaning, including hypothesis, speculation and supposition, by constructing sentences in varied ways.
What you need: Copies of *The Lion, the Witch and the Wardrobe*, Extract 1 on page 8, photocopiable page 30 and writing materials.

What to do

- Read Extract 1 together, highlighting phrases and rhetorical questions that indicate speculation about the validity of Lucy's story: *unless, we must assume, how could, if… then, even if, likely, so, on the other hand.*
- Point out how such words are essential if you want to discuss a hypothetical situation: a 'what if' or 'let us suppose' or 'for the sake of argument' (in the sense of discussion) matter. Explain that this is the same style of language and sentence structure used in all speculative conversation.
- Ask the children to discuss their beliefs with a partner. This can be at any level from *Do you believe there's a parallel universe?* to *Do you believe in fairies?* or *Are you superstitious?*
- After each has had a turn to express and explain their beliefs, hand out photocopiable page 30. Ask the children to write a few paragraphs explaining their belief, considering possible objections, and justifying their viewpoint, based on their notes.

Differentiation
For older/more confident learners: Challenge children to present their written argument as a brief presentation, answering questions or objections from others, adopting techniques similar to those used by the Professor: logical reasoning and rhetorical question.
For younger/less confident learners: Listen to children's conversations and prompt them to develop logical language by asking questions, such as *How do you explain…? What if…?*

By Jove, it's dated!

- Look at the language used in *The Lion, the Witch and the Wardrobe.*
- Think of a modern equivalent that you might use or hear today.

Write it in the column.

Mid-20th-century phrases and idioms	Early 21st-century translation
"Perfectly splendid!" (Chapter 1)	
"We've fallen on our feet and no mistake!" (Chapter 1)	
"There's a wireless…" (Chapter 1)	
"Rather!" (Chapter 2)	
"But it's pretty poor sport standing here in the snow." (Chapter 4)	
"Sharp's the word!" (Chapter 5)	
"Great Scott!" (Chapter 6)	
"By Jove!" (Chapter 8)	
"By gum!" (Chapter 12)	

- The children found a wireless when they arrived. What three items would you like to find if you were staying in an old house nowadays? Explain why.

1. ______________________________

2. ______________________________

3. ______________________________

Adapting true stories

- Write your own allegory based on a true-life story.
- You can change the characters' names and age and choose if they are male or female. You can also change the setting and the events but try to keep them similar to the original true story.

I am going to write an allegory of the true story of (who?)

___

Their true-life story is set (when and where?)

___

This is what happened.

___

___

This is the final outcome.

___

___

In my allegory, the main character will be (who?)

___

The setting will be (when and where?)

___

The similar events that take place will be (what?)

___

___

The similar outcome will be

___

___

What do you believe in?

- Write below something that you believe in, but that some people might not (such as 'I believe there is life on other planets').

- Why do you believe this to be true?

- Does everyone believe this? If not, why do they disagree?
List some arguments they might use to challenge your belief.

- Can you justify your belief? Give examples of events that have strengthened your conviction.

- Now, put together a three-paragraph account of your belief, based on your notes, on the back of this page. In paragraph one, explain your belief. In paragraph two, suggest why some people might disagree. In paragraph three, justify your belief, with examples if possible.

Here are some phrases you may find useful:

if... then...	even if	let's assume
experience suggests	on the other hand	how could
it seems (un)likely that	whenever	so/therefore

Assessment advice

Themes of good and evil are threaded into *The Lion, the Witch and the Wardrobe.* Asking individuals to offer examples of some of these themes will encourage children to think more deeply about the underlying themes and point to their recognition and understanding of these. For example, ask: *In what ways do loyalty and disloyalty come into the story? Is there a time when it is wrong to remain loyal? Which character(s) show mixed loyalties, and why?* Examine other moral themes, such as truthfulness, honour, forgiveness, courage, faithfulness and constancy. Discuss what motivates characters to behave as they do at different stages of the plot. Note how confident learners are to draw examples from the text and relate them to real life to support their opinions.

The author's voice recurs throughout the story, encouraging readers to adopt the characters' point of view and empathise with their feelings and situation. At the same time, the fast-moving narrative of this fantasy, skilfully combined with realism, offers scope for analysis of the author's storytelling techniques. Encouraging the children to spot how the narrative hangs together and affects the reader – the use of analogy and simile; the realistic dialogue – will reveal further aspects of their level of comprehension.

The moral high ground

Objective: To assess understanding of underlying themes, causes and points of view.
What you need: Copies of *The Lion, the Witch and the Wardrobe*, photocopiable page 32 and writing materials.

What to do

- Discuss in what ways *The Lion, the Witch and the Wardrobe* can be seen as adopting a high moral standpoint, showing up the difference between right and wrong. Ask the children if the child characters are strong. *If not, who shows signs of weakness, and how? Does Edmund eventually rise to the challenge to triumph over wrong-doing?*
- Ask questions about characters' behaviour at specific points in the story, such as, *When Peter confesses to Aslan, why does he say that he feels partly responsible for Edmund's bad behaviour?* (He admits that he has retained his anger towards Edmund, partly driving him back to the Witch.)
- Invite suggestions of selfless behaviour among the characters (from Lucy to the Beavers to Aslan's ultimate sacrifice). Assess their level of comprehension from the children's responses and ability to explain their reasons, or support with textual evidence.
- Explain that the photocopiable sheet asks the children about the underlying themes in *The Lion, the Witch and the Wardrobe*, and that if they need more space for their responses, they may continue on the back of the page.
- Hand out photocopiable page 32 for the children to complete. Supply copies of *The Lion, the Witch and the Wardrobe.*
- You may extend the assessment exercise, by asking for explanations for the children's choices of words ringed, such as: 'Lucy felt responsible for the faun's arrest, and felt honour-bound to undo the inadvertent harm she had caused; she was brave because she would be putting her own life in danger.'

The moral high ground

- Themes of good and evil run throughout *The Lion, the Witch and the Wardrobe.*
- Read the headings below, and give **two** examples of events that involve each of these areas. Explain which characters are involved.

Faith, belief and trust

1 ______________________________

2 ______________________________

Forgiveness

1 ______________________________

2 ______________________________

- For each the following events, ring **two** words that describe the character's actions or decisions.

Lucy insists on staying in Narnia to try and rescue Mr Tumnus.

responsible   irrational   exasperating   brave

Susan and Peter offer to stay with Lucy and help.

jealous   loyal   interfering   supportive

Edmund secretly leaves the others and tells tales to the witch-queen.

deceitful   thoughtful   selfish   clever

Mr Tumnus decides not to hand over Lucy to the White Witch.

brave   conscientious   cunning   forgetful

- You may use a dictionary to help you.